ESSENTIAL

Getting Started on the Internet

Time-saving books that teach specific skills to busy people, focusing on what really matters; the things that make a difference – the *essentials*. Other books in the Essentials series include:

Making Great Presentations

Writing Good Reports

Speaking in Public

Responding to Stress

Succeeding at Interviews

Solving Problems

Hiring People

Writing Great Copy

Making the Best Man's Speech

Feeling Good for No Reason

Making the Most of Your Time

For full details please send for a free copy of the latest catalogue.
See back cover for address.

The things that really matter about

Getting Started on the Internet

Irene Krechowiecka

ESSENTIALS

Published in 1999 by
How To Books Ltd, 3 Newtec Place,
Magdalen Road, Oxford OX4 1RE, United Kingdom
Tel: (01865) 793806   Fax: (01865) 248780
email: info@howtobooks.co.uk
www.howtobooks.co.uk

British Library Cataloguing in Publication Data.
A catalogue record for this book is available from
the British Library.

Edited by David Venner
Cover design by Shireen Nathoo Design
Produced for How To Books by Deer Park Productions
Typeset by PDQ Typesetting, Newcastle-under-Lyme, Staffordshire
Printed and bound in Great Britain

ESSENTIALS *is an imprint of*
How To Books

Contents

Preface

The only thing you can say with any certainty about the Internet is that it changes quickly. So it may seem contradictory to be writing a book, which is after all lasting and unchangeable once it's been produced, about a medium that is in many ways the exact opposite. It's true that you could find much of what's in here on the Internet itself and that information would be constantly updated for you. But how do you make a start?

The aim of this book is to first tempt you into using the Internet and then help you to get started. Sure the Internet keeps changing, but once you've understood the essentials you'll be able to make sense of these changes quickly and keep up to date with Internet developments as well as everything else from share prices to medical research. A slippery subject like this is more manageable if you concentrate on the techniques rather than the technicalities. This is a book of techniques.

One of the most interesting recent changes has been the growth in free Internet provision. Initially this meant no subscription fees, now there are several offers of free phone calls at off peak times too. This is being driven by companies who want to persuade us to shop on the web. Don't let that put you off if you've no interest in buying things electronically. Take what's on offer and use this book to explore all the other things you can do.

Every care has been taken to check the currency and accuracy of the information in this book, but inevitably things will change. Suggestions for alterations and additions are welcome and can be sent to:

irene.k@unforgettable.com

1 Understanding What It's All About

The Internet has revolutionised the way the world communicates and has something to offer everyone regardless of their age or interests.

The Internet has already had a profound effect on the way we learn, conduct research, buy goods and communicate. It's becoming as normal an activity as watching television.

You'll have heard that it's a place for finding bargains or for being swindled, that it's an essential learning tool or a danger to society's morals, that it leads to isolation and addiction or that it brings people together. You may be concerned about the costs and confused by talk of free access. This book guides you through the basics and helps you understand what the Internet is and is not and how you can benefit from all the amazing things it offers even if you don't own a computer!

Any book about the Internet soon dates. That's why you won't find great lists of sites in this book. Instead you'll learn the essentials that give you the knowledge and confidence to find your own useful places and keep up to date with developments and changes.

IS THIS YOU?

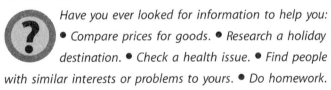

Have you ever looked for information to help you:
• Compare prices for goods. • Research a holiday destination. • Check a health issue. • Find people with similar interests or problems to yours. • Do homework.
• Move house. • Manage your finances. • Plan a journey.
• Understand your computer. • Check the latest news.
• Compare public services in your area with the rest of the country. • Find another job. • Give an effective presentation.
• Translate to or from another language. • Check the weather at home or in another part of the world. • Fill in a tax return.

UNDERSTANDING WHAT THE INTERNET IS

The Internet:

- is a network of computers linked by the telephone system,

- moves information around the world quickly and efficiently,

- enables people to share information and promote understanding, allows free speech, encourages learning and the exchange of ideas, and

- allows the unscrupulous to exploit vulnerabilities, invade privacy and defraud.

The most popular areas of the Internet are the **World Wide Web, email** and **news and discussion groups**.

No matter where you live the Internet can give you access to information from all parts of the world on all subjects. Whatever you want to know you will find information easily, cheaply and at any time of the day or night.

Guillain-Barré Syndrome

A guide for patients, relatives and friends.

The Guillain-Barré Syndrome Patient in
Intensive Care

A guide for relatives and friends.

Childhood Guillain-Barré
Syndrome

A guide for parents and
carers.

Medical information from reliable
sources is easily found. This comes from
http://www.gbs.org.uk

The World Wide Web is a glossy multimedia magazine, with text, pictures, sounds and videos. Use it for academic research or shopping, to find a job or holiday, to download games or research your family tree. It is made up of information provided by countless individuals and organisations. In theory you can find everything you would ever want with the click of a mouse. Information is linked in a way that gives it a web-like structure; by following links you go to related information. This can sometimes mean going round in circles and feeling trapped and frustrated! You need to spend a little time developing efficient search techniques in order to utilise the tremendous potential it offers.

Anyone can make a web site, millions do. Finding information is not difficult. Finding that which is worthwhile take a little practice and inside information. This book shows you how.

Email allows you to send messages, files, pictures, film clips and sounds to anyone else with an email address. It's a quick, cheap and efficient way of keeping in touch with people in the same building or at the other end of the world. You can stack up messages so that they all go together, and it's surprising how many you can send for one call unit. They take the same time to send regardless of their destination and can arrive almost instantly.

News and discussion groups are places where people with similar interests can discuss matters. You can listen in on discussions, contribute to them or start new ones on just about any subject you can think of.

 ## UNDERSTANDING WHAT THE INTERNET IS NOT

The Internet is such a newsworthy activity it leads to lots of misconceptions.

Either all good or all bad.

The Internet gives everyone an opportunity to have their say. There's no real censorship and no one controls it, so you get a mixture of everything that's out there. The good stuff far outweighs the bad, and you're in control of what you look at and what you choose to contribute.

Just for computer experts.

You don't have to know anything about computers to be able to use the Internet. If you can handle a mouse you can explore the offerings of the world.

Very expensive to use.

If you already have a computer the only other cost you need incur is your phone charges. There are lots of ways of keeping these to a minimum as you'll see in this book. Using email instead of post, phone or fax will save you money. There are many bargains to be found through the Internet. If you know where to look it can be one of the most cost and time effective ways of getting what you need.

The answer to everything.

The Internet is not always the best tool to use. It's an additional resource amongst all the others you're already using.

③ KNOWING WHAT YOU NEED

All you need is an interest in finding out more. You don't even have to own a computer – if you're uncertain whether the Internet has anything to offer you, try it out first using public access.

If you decide to go for personal Internet access you need a **computer** with a **modem, browser software** and a **phone**. It's also possible to access the Internet through your **television**, although this is more limited and less flexible than using a computer. A **computer** bought recently will probably have everything you need to connect to the Internet. If your computer does not have a modem you can buy one for less than £100. If you are using an older computer check that its speed and memory will be able to cope with the demands you'll be putting on it. The companies which provide the service that connects you to the Internet (**Internet Service Providers**) generally recommend a minimum of 16 MB of Ram and 80 MB of hard disc space. Most computers bought over the last few years will have this.

The **modem** allows computers to communicate with each other through the phone system. The faster your modem and computer are, the quicker you will receive and send information. This minimises time spent connected to the phone (**online**) which usually has a cost attached to it.

The most reliable sources of up to date information on equipment are articles and adverts in the many Internet magazines. These are available in paper form or on the web.

A modem can also act as an answering and fax machine when linked to your computer. This is independent of the Internet and a valuable extra resource, so check for these facilities.

Your modem connects into your phone line. The easiest way

is to get a 'doubler' for your phone and plug your modem and phone into the same line. Because the one line is shared you will not be able to use both at the same time. If you need to use both simultaneously you have to install an extra line.

In addition to this hardware you need software called a **web browser**. The two most commonly used are **Netscape Navigator** and **Microsoft's Internet Explorer**. Both are free products and one or both may already be on your computer. If not you should be able to get one as part of a free start up package from any Internet Service Provider (ISP). You need an account with one to connect to the Internet. Some organisations charge a monthly fee, but a growing number offer such services for free. Detailed information on web browsers and ISPs can be found in Chapter 2.

Television Internet access is relatively new to the UK and uses your TV and phone to connect to the Internet. It's not as flexible as computer based access, as the system has no memory so you cannot store information or work offline. However, its big advantage is that you don't have to buy a computer. All the equipment you need is supplied by the provider and they will upgrade that as necessary. There's a monthly charge for using the service which is subject to taking out a 12 month contract and spending an agreed minimum on phone calls. The main provider at the time of writing is **NTL** in conjunction with **Virgin Net** and they can be contacted on **0800 052 4321**.

 ACCESSING THE INTERNET WITHOUT YOUR OWN COMPUTER

If you want to try out the Internet before buying personal

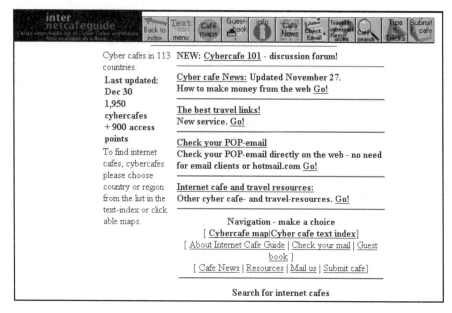

Once you're on the Internet you can find cybercafes in all corners of the world from http://www.netcafeguide.com

equipment, or if you know you will only use it occasionally, there are a number of places that offer public access. It's a cheap way to find out more and often comes with help and technical support thrown in.

Places to try:

Many **libraries** offer Internet access and short courses to get you started. They normally charge around £5 an hour. **Cybercafes** are places where you can eat, drink and access the Internet. You'll find them in *Yellow Pages*, usually listed under computer services.

Some **primary** and **secondary schools** are offering Internet access to the public. This is normally outside school hours and can be linked to training and child care. Check with your Local Education Authority.

Many **universities** make facilities available to the public in conjunction with short courses to help you get started.

There are a number of **local and national schemes promoting computer literacy**. In the UK an initiative called *IT For All* offers a free, easy to read guide on all aspects of information technology and details of courses and computer access points in your locality. Contact them on **0800 456 567**.

The BBC, for example, run **national campaigns** such as *Web Wise* and *Computers Don't Bite*. These include TV programmes to help you see what computers can do for you and events such as free 'taster sessions' in libraries, shopping centres, buses and pubs.

Friends and relatives with Internet access are often happy to share their discoveries with you, particularly if you cover the phone costs for time you spend online.

MAKING WHAT MATTERS WORK FOR YOU

✓ Check with your local library or ring *IT For All* 0800 456 567 to get details of public Internet provision and starter courses in your area.

✓ Arrange an 'Introduction to the Internet' session to see it for yourself.

✓ If you have a computer see what extra you would need to connect it to the Internet.

✓ If you have access to the Internet check details of cybercafes at **http://www.netcafeguide.com**

2 Getting Started

It doesn't cost much to get connected to the Internet. The software is free and a growing number of Internet Service Providers no longer charge a fee. Once you've sorted out your connection, you need to acquaint yourself with your browser software.

1 **CHOOSING AN INTERNET SERVICE PROVIDER**

2 **UNDERSTANDING YOUR BROWSER**

things that
really matter

If you have your own computer and want to set up a personal Internet account there are lots of companies to choose from. Increasingly they offer access to the Internet for free, and compete for customers to give their product away to! This is a fast moving area with daily changes and developments, and the web is a great way of keeping up to date with what's happening.

The software you use for accessing the Internet is easy to use, and lets you do much more than just look at web pages. This chapter shows what to look for when choosing an Internet Service Provider and how to quickly familiarise yourself with your browser so you can use the web efficiently and get the most out of it for the least effort and cost.

IS THIS YOU?

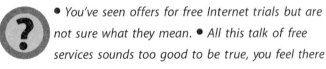

• You've seen offers for free Internet trials but are not sure what they mean. • All this talk of free services sounds too good to be true, you feel there has to be a catch. • Everyone's telling you it's simple to connect but you're not convinced. • You pay for your Internet access and wonder if you should switch to a free provider. • Your computer has Internet software loaded but you're not sure what to do with it.

① CHOOSING AN INTERNET SERVICE PROVIDER

Internet Service Providers (ISPs) are commercial organisations which link you to the Internet through their computers. When you connect to the Internet your first call is to your ISP and should only be a local call. They connect you to the rest of the world.

There are a growing number of companies who provide free access to the Internet. What they offer has very few differences from companies that charge a monthly fee. One of the largest is Freeserve from the Dixons Group. This is a full Internet access service with no registration or subscription fees and no hourly on line charges. It gives unlimited access to the Internet, newsgroups, unlimited email addresses as well as space to create your own web site. Installation CDs can be picked up from any Dixons, Currys, PC World or The Link stores. Other free providers include Tesco, Arsenal Football Club, Virgin Net and British Telecom.

Look out for free off peak Internet call offers from ISPs who team up with telecom companies. However, before switching to one of these try them out alongside your existing provider. Services with free off peak phone numbers

Net 4 Nowt

Brought to you by Paul Hillbeck and *QiQ*

News	Main Content	Features
Get Paid As You Surf	THE ISP DIRECTORY	The Cable & Wireless 50p Offer
CurrantBun hacked	A - C	You use lots of free e-mail services?
	D - F	Pop 3 Scan Mailbox could be for you!
French Unlimited Internet	G - M	Try here or here!
	N - S	
AOL's new free ISP	T - Z	UK Free ISP FAQ
		By Paul Roberts
European ISP Market to Consolidate	Our latest site changes	
		Vocaltel update
FreeServe revolution rolls on	The latest free call ISPs	
		Vote for your favourite ISP and now...
AOL to go free?	Other listings of free ISPs	vote for the WORST
	Search the site	
Earlier News Stories		Discusson Forum
	Contact Us	

There are now 170 Free ISPs listed

To keep up to date with who's offering what and how good it is
take a look at Net 4 Nowt http://www.n4n.co.uk

can be permanently engaged or painfully slow to transmit data.

The main differences between free and priced services are:

- The cost of calls to their helpline. Most fee charging providers use local or national call rate numbers. Free providers can charge up to £1 a minute. However, many have extensive on line help and offer additional support through email and newsgroups so you can sort problems out easily once you're on line.

- Access to pre-selected content. Many providers hope to retain paying customers by providing extra services exclusive to members, such as news, travel, educational

and weather information. These can offer an easy
introduction to the web as they select and categorise
sites for you, as well as offering general Internet access.
However, content-rich services like Virgin now offer free
Internet access.

When choosing a provider **important factors to check
are**:

- That their software is compatible with your system. Some
  free providers don't have Mac compatible software, or
  require the latest operating system. If you need to buy a
  new computer to make use of a free service then it
  might not be quite the bargain it first appears. However,
  with the growing number of free providers you should
  be able to find one that matches your requirements.

- The type of email connection included. Some free
  providers only offer web based email, which means you
  have to be on line to compose and read mail. It's better
  to get a POP 3 mail account (see Chapter 6).

- Whether there are restrictions on business use. Some
  free providers stipulate personal use only.

- The availability of on line or email help. This is
  particularly important if their helpline is expensive to
  access.

- That the speed of their modems matches the speed of
  yours. If not transfers could be slow.

- The ratio of modems to users they have. If it is high e.g.
  1:20, they may be engaged when you try to get through.
  A ratio of 1:10 is fairly standard. The lower it is, the
  better.

- How many newsgroups they give access to, it's often in
  excess of 30,000.

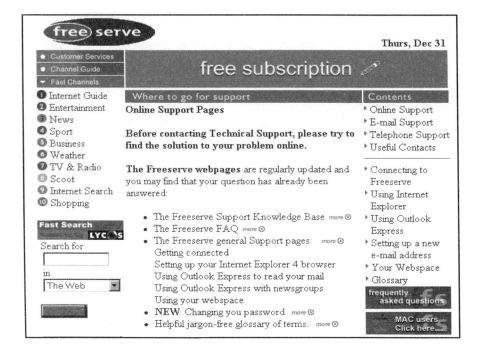

Freeserve (http://www.freeserve.net) offers selected content and excellent on line help.

- If they offer free web space. You may wish to create your own web page – it's surprisingly easy!

- What advantages a priced provider offers you over a free one and how much that is worth to you.

- How they deal with help line enquiries. Several that offer cheap call rate access combine this with the expensive practice of answering the phone promptly, offering you a long list of pre-recorded choices, then playing soothing music interspersed with frequent apologies for keeping you waiting. To be avoided!

- The minimum subscription period. Some ask for a whole year's subscription. You should not do this without trying them out first. If you choose this option check how long they've been in the business and what happens to your annual subscription if they go out of business, or decide to make their service free.

You'll be able to get answers to these questions from the company's customer service department, the store you get your free software from or their web site. If you opt for a service with a fee, use free trials before you decide who to sign up with. You can then compare the additional features they offer and see which suits your needs. A free trial is only free in terms of the cost of using their computers, you still have to pay for the phone call time. 'Unlimited free access' means access to their computers.

 UNDERSTANDING YOUR BROWSER

You should explore the functions of your browser software before you connect to the Internet. Work offline to familiarise yourself with its layout and commands.

Browser software enables you to move around web pages. The most commonly used ones, **Netscape Navigator** and **Internet Explorer**, are free. Internet Explorer 5 (IE5) is used in the screen shots in this book, but its appearance and functions are common to other browsers. Like everything else associated with the Internet, browsers are continually being upgraded.

New versions offer more facilities than old ones, some are really useful additions, others are not. Version 5 of Explorer (IE5) for example offers:

- file saving options that retain all features of a web page,
- better offline working facilities,
- enhanced search options,
- sophisticated mail and news filtering.

It is not necessary to have the most up to date browser. In some cases an older computer may not be powerful enough to run the latest software.

If you want to keep up with developments look at **http://www.browsers.com**

Web pages

You can look at browser software and previously visited web pages without being online. Spending time offline getting used to the layout and functions of your browser costs nothing. Then when you go on line, you will be familiar with the common commands and able to work quickly.

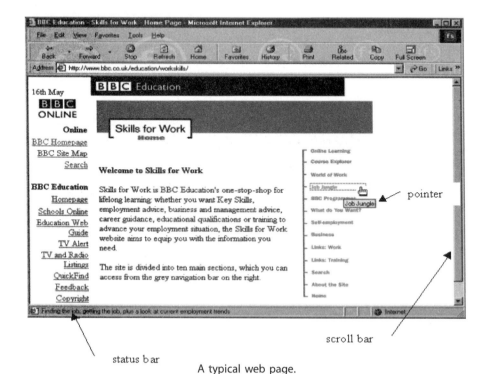

A typical web page.

The commands for your browser are at the top of your screen. As text may take up more space than your screen can display, you can use the **scroll bar** or **page down key** to move through it.

Your **pointer** is used to move around the screen. Use it to click on words, images, or the scroll bar. Links to other pages or sites are usually coloured, underlined text or a picture.

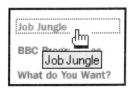

The pointer changes from an arrow to a hand when it is placed over a link.

At the bottom is a **status bar** that lets you know what's going on. If you hover over a link, a summary of its content or its address will appear so you can see what clicking on that link will take you to. In this case it's another page on the same site, but it could be to another site anywhere in the world.

Using the commands

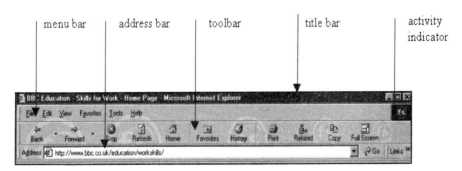

Older browsers do not have features such as Related and History.

- The **title bar** has the name of the page you are viewing plus the minimise, restore and close buttons.

- The **address bar** gives you the URL of the web page you are viewing. Typing the URL in the address bar takes you to that web page. If you follow a link, the new URL will be shown here.

On the newest browsers you can type your search phrase in the address bar and find links to explore.

- The **activity indicator** becomes animated when data is being transmitted.

The **toolbar** provides quick links to popular commands from the menu bar. The commands are activated by a single click of the mouse. When they are not available to you the icons are 'greyed out'. Here the toolbar is in picture and text form, but can also be displayed as just pictures or just text.

- The **back** button takes you to the previous page you were viewing.

- The **forward** button can only be used after going back.

- The **stop** button is useful when transfers are taking too long and you wish to terminate a connection. Keep an eye on the status bar at the bottom of the screen to see the progress of transmissions. Your modem may have the potential to operate at impressive speeds, but information is sometimes received at less than 1% of its capability.

- The **refresh** button reloads your current page. This is useful if a transfer of information has been interrupted or corrupted or you want to update it.

- The **home** button takes you to your home page. This is the first page you connect to when you access the web. It is normally set by the ISP to take you to their site, but you can change it to a page of your choice either on the web or from your existing computer files. You can choose to always open your browser with a blank page (see page 28).

- The **favourites** button opens up a list of sites you've previously added. You can go back to sites on this list

Which buttons your toolbar displays is easy to change. Click the right button of your mouse anywhere in the toolbar and explore the Customize... option

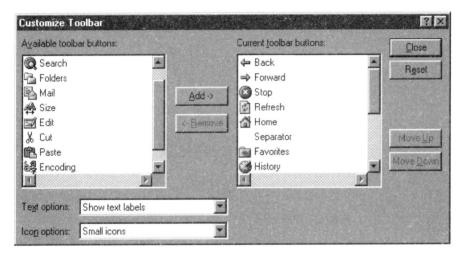

On newer browsers the toolbar can be customised.

with a single click of the mouse.

- The **history** button shows a list of recently visited sites. You can use it for offline browsing (see Chapter 4).

- The **print** button prints the current web page. A web page can be several screen or paper pages long. To print specific pages only use **file/print** from the menu bar.

- The **related** button will bring up a list of sites that are similar to the one you are currently viewing.

- The **copy** button places highlighted text or graphics on the clipboard allowing you to insert it in other applications.

- The **fullscreen** button allows the web page to take up all of the screen.

- The **search** button was not selected but if you choose to use it, it will connect you to the search tool selected by your provider. See Chapter 5 for information on effective searching.

Commands in the **menu bar** enable you to carry out a range of functions. Experiment with these by working off line on any previously viewed page. Some to try include:

File/save as... allows you to save a page and is one way of later using that information offline. IE5 offers a 'save web page complete' option. In earlier browsers this command saves the text only and pictures need to be saved separately (see Chapter 4).

File/work offline allows you to look at previously visited pages without connecting to the phone. You find these using the **history** button. Not all pages in your history will

Clicking on an unavailable link will bring up a dialogue box that gives you the option to reconnect to the Internet.

be available for viewing in offline mode. If your pointer changes to a hand with a no entry sign that link cannot be viewed offline. The same symbol appears if you try to follow a link you did not previously access.

The title bar tells you when you are working offline and a modem with cross symbol appears in the status bar.

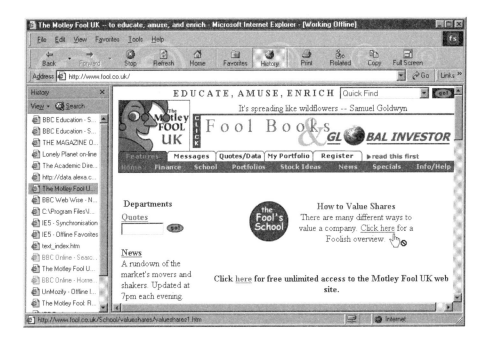

Experiment with the Search and View facilities in History – they make offline browsing quick and easy.

Selecting the **work offline** option when you are connected to the Internet **does not disconnect you from the phone**. It simply allows you to work on files stored as temporary Internet files without trying to connect to the Internet. This option needs to be selected for you to be able to view files in the history folder. To make sure you are offline, disconnect using the computer's dialler or pull the modem lead out of the phone connection. Software that enables comprehensive and flexible offline working with older browsers is described in Chapter 4.

File/send allows you to send the page you are viewing as an email.

Edit functions here are similar to any word processing package. You can **select** and **copy** text and graphics to other applications. There's also a **find** option which allows

you to search long documents for a particular word or phrase.

View gives you a drop down menu which allows you to choose which toolbars are displayed and in what format; whether or not to include the status or explorer bars. The history window on the left side of the web page shown on page 27 is an **explorer bar**. You can alter text size and look at the source code of the document you are viewing. The **go to, stop, refresh** and **full screen** options have the same effect as clicking one of the toolbar buttons.

The menu from the **favourites** option allows you to bookmark the page you're looking at or go to one you've added to favourites. Details are in the next chapter.

Tools/Internet options allows you to manage your Internet access in the way that suits you. This is where you go to control the way your web pages look, the way the Internet is accessed and to clean up temporary Internet files. Detailed explanations are in Chapter 4.

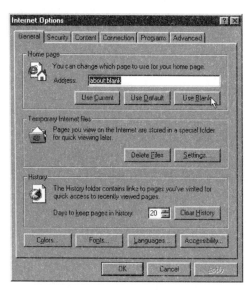

One setting worth changing early on is your choice of **home page**. It will have been set to connect you to the website of your ISP, so every time you open up your browser it will start to dial up. If you want to start by working offline, the simplest way is to set your home page as a blank. The command for this is on the **general** tab of **Internet options**.

It's easy to use a blank home page.

All the software has **help** sections. You can print the pages that deal with relevant topics and explore your browser's operations without being online.

MAKING WHAT MATTERS WORK FOR YOU

✓ Pick up installation software for a selection of free service providers and compare what they offer. These are available from their stores or web sites.

✓ Check your system has the necessary space and memory to cope before you install any programs.

✓ If you already have an Internet connection check how providers compare by visiting their web sites:
http://www.arsenal.co.uk
http://www.clara.net
http://www.cwcom.net
http://www.demon.net
http://www.freeserve.net
http://www.lineone.net
http://www.localtel.co.uk
http://www.tesco.net
http://www.virgin.net

✓ Keep up to date with new services and compare free providers using **Net 4 Nowt. http://www.n4n.co.uk.**

✓ If you want to try a subscription service, use one that offers a free trial.

✓ Before you connect to the web spend some time looking at your browser to get a feel for where the commands are and what they do.

✓ Set a blank page as your home page.

✓ Try some sites to get a feel of what's out there. Simply type some of the following in the address bar and press the enter key.
http://www.bbc.co.uk
http://www.buy.co.uk
http://www.fool.co.uk
http://www.jobsunlimited.co.uk
http://www.lonelyplanet.com
http://www.upmystreet.com

✓ Once you're connected to a site follow any links that interest you. Set yourself a limit of ten minutes connection time.

✓ When you disconnect select **File/Work Offline** and click on your history button. Revisit pages at your leisure to explore your browser's functions.

✓ Try out all your toolbar buttons and explore the menu bar.

3 Being in Control

The store of information on the Internet is huge.
You need to be able to manage and evaluate it.

4

things that
really matter

1 **UNDERSTANDING URLs**

2 **WORKING WITH FAVOURITES**

3 **KEEPING SAFE**

4 **EVALUATING INFORMATION**

New technologies make finding information easier than ever before. You need to be organised in choosing what you look at and what you keep.

Look at all information critically – a good looking site is no guarantee of quality. Many of the best sites are relatively plain. Before you start using the Internet you should be aware of its potential dangers and how to minimise them.

The Internet is a great free for all and consequently the quality of information varies enormously. On river pollution for example you'll find pages by individuals, primary school projects, reports from environmental agencies, academic contributions and much more. Decide what sort of information you want and who is likely to provide it.

Understanding how web site addresses are made up can help with this. Once you find the right sources of information it's easy to keep their details for easy access through your browser's bookmarking facility.

IS THIS YOU?

 • Overwhelmed by information on the web? • Not sure which sites are worth spending time on? • Frustrated by error messages that tell you the page is not available? • Trying to remember the address of an excellent site you once visited? • Worried about your child's use of the Internet? • Concerned about people invading your privacy? • Interested in buying something on line but unsure how safe it is?

UNDERSTANDING URLs

Every web page has a unique address known as its **Uniform Resource Locator** or **URL**. These are a cross between a phone number and an address. You need the same complete accuracy when using them, one character wrong and you end up somewhere else. However, like addresses you can read them and learn something about their destination. If you understand what makes up a URL you can try put it right if it doesn't work. It also gives you clues about who's providing the information which is important when evaluating how accurate and worthwhile that information is.

At its simplest a URL looks like this:

http: Stands for **hypertext transfer protocol**. It is always followed by :// It tells your browser what type of document you want. For normal web documents you do not need to enter it as part of the address, the browser assumes that if you enter nothing, http:// should be there. Other commonly used protocols are ftp:// and news://. Secure sites start with https://

www.fool. This is known as the **domain name** and tells you the name of the server and company/organisation/individual.

co. Tells you what sort of organisation it is. Commonly used ones are:

ac.	=	academic institution in the UK only. Elsewhere it's denoted by edu.
co.	=	commercial company in the UK
com.	=	commercial company elsewhere and increasingly in the UK
gov.	=	governmental organisation
org.	=	other types of organisation
sch.	=	school site
net.	=	internet service provider

uk This tells you in which country the site originates. Every country has its own code, e.g. fr = France; is = Iceland; ie = Ireland; za = South Africa; pl = Poland; de = Germany. USA web sites do not normally use a country code. Resist the temptation to put a full stop at the end of a URL, there never is one!

The basic URL will generally take you to the **home page** of a web site. These provide content lists or site maps to help you find your way around the site.

URLs that extend beyond the country code are the addresses of **specific pages** or **files**.

They are separated from the main body of the URL by a / (forward slash). This is a German (**de**) recruitment agency called Jobware and this page gives information on vacancies they have in Africa.

This URL has a ~ (**tilde**). These are often used for

| Address | http://www.nottingham.ac.uk/~brzslweb/allsorts/ODInfo.htm |

personal directories which can move or change. This page is from Nottingham University's web site and contains information on Open Days. When specific files like these move you get an error message. If this happens edit the URL in the address bar to remove everything to the right of the country indicator. Here that would leave you with the address **http://www.nottingham.ac.uk** the site's home page. You can then use the site's index or search facility to find the information you need.

If you are arriving at a new site from a link, you may be taken to specific files deep within it. It's always a good idea to see who owns the site and what its purpose is. If there are links to a Home Page or About Us section use them, if not alter the URL in the address box to take you to the home page.

② WORKING WITH FAVOURITES

Develop the habit of bookmarking sites you want to revisit.

Add to Favorites...
Organize Favorites...
📁 Sites to visit
📁 Careers
📁 Guardian
📁 Employers
📁 Net That Course
📁 Net That Job
📁 Personal
📁 Search tools

Be ruthless about deleting links you no longer use.

Bookmarking a page means adding its URL to a list so you can go back to it without re-typing the address. If you're looking at a site you want to visit again add it to your favourites using that option on the menu bar. The drop down box also allows you to organise your favourites and this should be done offline. Well organised favourites make it quick and easy to revisit sites but it's easy for your lists to grow out of control.

When viewing documents on or off line use the right button technique described in Chapter 4 to add URLs of links you'd like to explore later. Create a folder called Sites to Visit and put the new ones in here for next time you go online.

 KEEPING SAFE

The dangers of the Internet are well reported and put many people off using it. However, like all aspects of life, an understanding of the risks helps you minimise them. If you are aware of the dangers and safeguards that exist to protect you, you can make Internet use as safe as any other activity.

Personal safety

The Internet is both personal and anonymous. The people you communicate with can hide or protect their identity behind an email address or chat line alias and so can you. There is no problem until you start to divulge personal

A Parents' Guide to the Internet

nch action for children

Help to make the Net a safer place

House Rules

There is a PDF of the full booklet 'Children on the Internet Opportunities and Hazards' [272K].

If you need to download Adobe Acrobat Reader use this button [this will open a new window].

internet@ction

Download this comprehensive guide to Internet safety.

details. Take the usual precautions you would when dealing with any stranger. Remember that people online may not be what they seem. Because you can't see or hear the person it would be easy for someone to misrepresent him or herself. Thus, someone indicating that she is a 14-year-old girl could in reality be a 50-year-old man.

There is excellent practical advice available from a range of organisations who are promoting Internet use as a safe and positive experience for all. The above is from **http://www.nchafc.org.uk**; further sources of help and advice are listed at the end of the chapter. For details of how to use **PDF files** see Chapter 4.

In the UK, **The Internet Watch Foundation http://www.iwf.org.uk** exists to address the problem of illegal material on the Internet. Their particular concern is child pornography, but they encourage Internet users to report any material that appears illegal. Their web site offers the facility to report material and there is a hotline you can contact.

Only illegal material can be removed. However, there is much that is technically legal but nevertheless highly offensive. Rating systems and blocking software to filter out such materials are widely available.

Financial safety

Commercial fraud that existed before the Internet exists now on it. New technologies enable new ways of perpetrating and combating fraud.

Microsoft's Content Advisor, an integral part of Internet Explorer, provides a basic filter.

Anyone can set up a web site and claim to be whatever takes their fancy. Sites offering goods and services for sale number millions. Some belong to reputable companies and individuals, others to dishonest and dubious operators. It's up to you to check that the companies you are dealing with are legitimate and that any money you part with is safe. Electronic transactions are subject to the same framework of domestic and international rules as traditional means of shopping including, for example, existing rules on distance selling (such as mail order), advertising and consumer credit.

Secure sites have an unbroken key or padlock symbol and the URL starts with https.

 Financial transactions on the web should only be carried out on **secure sites**.

Sending credit card details by email is not safe, it's like putting them on a postcard. Browsers use **SSL** (Secure Sockets Layer) to encrypt data you send so it cannot be read or changed during transmission. Using a secure site is as safe as giving your credit card details over the phone. It  doesn't remove all the risks. You are trusting the server administrator with your credit card number and no technology can protect you from dishonest or careless people. One great advantage of paying by credit card is that if you do not get the services or goods you paid for you may be reimbursed. It's not advisable to carry out financial transactions on computers that are for public access. Someone could see your credit card details as you enter them or later retrieve the page with them on from the computer's cache.

Another worry is that you don't get what you expect. If the company or product is new to you, take the same precautions as you would when buying over the phone or by mail order. Sites could be set up for the purpose of collecting credit card numbers and not send anything. Check for alternative ways of contacting the supplier such as phone, fax or physical address in case something goes wrong.

Computer safety

A **computer virus** is a piece of code designed to disrupt the operation of a computer. Files containing viruses can be transmitted across the Internet through file downloads or mail attachments. Your browser will normally display a **warning** when you're about to download the type of file that could contain a virus. You'll be asked whether you want to open the file or save it to disk.

Viruses are usually hidden in programs and activated when the programs run. It's essential to install software that

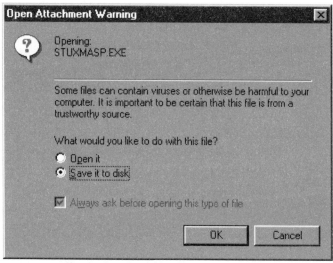

To protect yourself only download files from sources that you know are safe.

checks for viruses before you download anything from the web or open an email attachment. If you have a virus it can sometimes be cleaned up by this software. To get full protection make sure you run the program as recommended and update it regularly.

 EVALUATING INFORMATION

Worthwhile sites state their purpose clearly but there are still things to check like:

- Who owns the site?
- What's their main purpose – selling, educating or entertaining?
- Would you trust this company/individual/organisation to provide accurate, reliable information in real life?
- When was the information last updated?
- What information can you find about the author?

You should also be sceptical of sites where:

- There is no information on who owns the site or its purpose.
- There is no contact information.
- There is no date for when the information was produced or updated.
- Information is poorly presented.

Remember that very little information is truly objective. 'Reputable' sources such as universities, government departments, newspapers, broadcasters, learned societies and publishers have sites with information which is comprehensive, accurate and up to date, but they all have a point of view they are trying to promote.

MAKING WHAT MATTERS WORK FOR YOU

✓ Add a few links to your favourites to see how it works. These don't have to be web pages, they could be word processing documents, spreadsheets or any file on your computer. Organise your favourites or bookmarks. Create new folders and move individual links.

✓ Find out more about personal safety on the Internet by visiting the following sites:
http://www.iwf.org.uk
http://www.nchafc.org.uk
http://www.netparents.org
http://www.safesurf.com
http://www.smartparent.com
http://www.worldvillage.com/wv/school/html/control.htm

✓ Get yourself an up to date virus check program.

✓ Explore the filtering offered by Internet Explorer's Content Advisor. Use **tools/internet options...** and the **content** tab in the dialogue box.

✓ Go through the motions of ordering something from a web site to see a secure connection. The Internet Bookshop
http://www.bookshop.co.uk provides a good example of this.

✓ Look at all information from the Internet critically using this checklist:
  ✓ Does it come from a trustworthy source?
  ✓ What are the author's credentials?
  ✓ Is it up to date?
  ✓ Is it suitable for your purpose?
  ✓ Does it make any bias clear?
  ✓ Is there contact information?

4 Becoming Proficient

As you gain confidence with Internet use there are a few extra things it's worth mastering to help you get the most from the web.

5

things that really matter

1 USING THE RIGHT BUTTON OF THE MOUSE

2 MANAGING YOUR OPTIONS

3 DOWNLOADING FILES AND PROGRAMS

4 WORKING OFFLINE

5 KEEPING COSTS DOWN

It's easy to develop good browsing habits that significantly reduce the time you spend connected to the phone and help you get the most from the sites you visit. Browser software is user friendly and offers the potential to do a lot more than just connect to web sites. You can for example copy text and graphics from web pages and use them in other applications.

If you don't like the way web pages are displayed the chances are you'll be able to change it. Don't be afraid to experiment and change settings to suit yourself.

Use the Internet to get new software to help with all the applications on your computer. There's an amazing number of things available completely free and most priced programs have a **try before you buy** option.

Indiscriminate use of the Internet can lead to huge phone bills. An understanding of how things work and where to find what you need can help you keep costs to a minimum.

IS THIS YOU?

• You're confused by menus that sometimes pop up on your web page. • You find some of the colours on web pages difficult to read on screen or print out and would like to make things plainer. • You'd like to know how to turn off pictures and animations that slow your computer down and be able to turn them back on again. • You'd like to download files and programs but are not sure what this means. • You've downloaded a file but can't open it. • You're concerned about your phone bills. • You've heard about working offline but don't know how to. • You're worried that Internet use could develop into an expensive addiction.

USING THE RIGHT BUTTON OF THE MOUSE

To **activate** a **command** you normally click with the left button of the mouse. With current browser software clicking the right button of the mouse will bring up an options menu which enables you to carry out extra functions. The

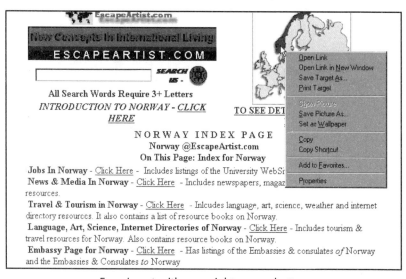

Experiment with your right mouse button.

right click is context sensitive, which means you get different options depending where on the screen you click. Here the pointer is on an image that acts as a link to another web page and the menu has options to allow you to do things with the link and the image. Right clicking on a text link brings up a menu with all the link but none of the picture options.

- **Open link** takes you to the new web page, clicking with the left button of the mouse on the image or linking text would do the same.

- **Open link in new window** opens a fresh browser page to display the new page and keeps the current page open. You can have several browser windows open at once but this may tax the computer's memory and cause your machine to slow down or crash.

- **Save target as ...** allows you to save the linked page without opening it first.

- **Print target** allows you to print the linked page without opening it first.

- **Show picture** is greyed out here because the picture is already shown.

- **Save picture as ...** allows you to save that image.

- **Set as wallpaper** lets you use that image as your backdrop.

- **Copy** puts the picture on your clipboard.

- **Copy shortcut** places the URL of the linked site on your clipboard.

- **Add to favourites ...** puts the URL of the linking site into your favourites file.

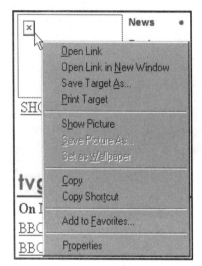

You need to be connected to the Internet to open and save links, print or view target. All the other functions can be done offline.

If you choose not to display pictures an icon appears instead of the picture. You can use it as a link and have all the same options for saving, printing and copying. You can choose to load a particular picture. **Show Picture** would display this one picture only, not others on the page.

A click with the right button of the mouse in the main body of a page will bring up a menu box with the most popular commands from the toolbar. Some users find this a quicker way to move around the web than using the top toolbar. If the page you're viewing has a background design there will be the option to save or copy the background.

② MANAGING YOUR OPTIONS

The way your browser displays pictures and text is not fixed, change it to suit your preferences and needs.

You can manage how you access the Internet and how web pages look by choosing **Internet options ...** from the **tools** command on the menu bar. Spend some time offline looking at this and trying out different settings.

From the **general** tab you can:

- change the colours web pages use,
- clean up your web cache from time to time by deleting temporary Internet files,
- decide how long you want to keep files in the history section and clear it out periodically,

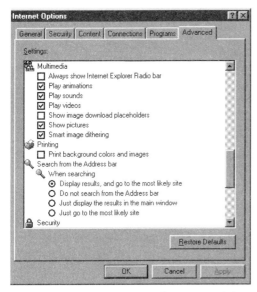

* use the **accessibility ...** option to have pages displayed with the font, colour and background you find easiest to use.

From the **advanced** tab you can:

* turn images, animations, videos and sounds off and on,

* change the appearance of your toolbar

* disable printing of background colours and images.

Before you alter anything make a note of the default setting so you can put things back as they were. Some sections have a Restore Defaults that does this for you.

 DOWNLOADING FILES AND PROGRAMS

As well as providing information, many web pages give you the option of **downloading** files. These can be documents, pictures, videos or programs. Once you've downloaded a file it's stored on your computer. Programs available may be **freeware** or **shareware**. Freeware is completely free, shareware normally gives you a free evaluation period after which you need to pay to continue to use the program.

If you're downloading a file you need to check that you have the software to open it. Common formats include document files (**DOC**) for Microsoft Word, and Portable Document Format (**PDF**) which requires **Adobe Acrobat Reader** to open it. This can be downloaded for free from the web. The main site can be accessed at **www.adobe.com**

Program files are often sent in a compressed or zipped

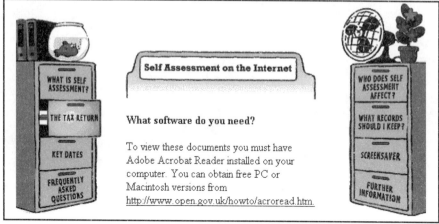

Pages offering pdf files usually include a link to an Adobe download site.

format, which makes transmission faster. The standard program for dealing with these zip files is WinZip and available as a free download from **www.winzip.com**

Downloading files is a simple point and click operation, all you need to do is decide which directory you want to save your file in. A dialogue box appears as you're downloading and shows progress. Keep an eye on this and if it's taking too long, cancel and try again at less busy time.

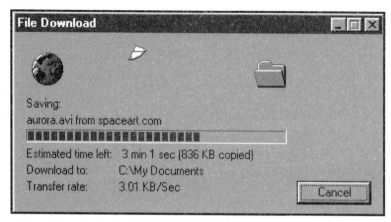

Always virus check programs you've downloaded before running them.

WORKING OFFLINE

You can significantly reduce the time you spend connected to the phone by always reading and printing documents offline. Any web page you visit is stored in the computer's memory cache for a time. The help section of your web browser software will tell you how to regulate the size of the cache. You can open cached files without being connected to the phone. On newer browsers the **history** facility enables you to work offline, see page 25. If you want to save sections of your cache or are using an older browser then investigate offline reading software. Offline browsers process the cache into an index which retains the original file names and URLs. You can follow any links that you visited whilst on line. Images are retained within the processed web pages.

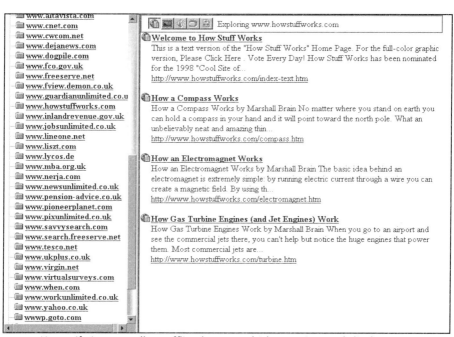

Unmozify is an excellent offline browser which organises and displays your cache efficiently for offline use. Download a 30 day evaluation copy from http://www.evolve.co.uk

KEEPING COSTS DOWN

1.   Check on free Internet access provision

The number of free providers is growing. Check what each offers, particularly the system requirements and hidden costs. Go for one with **POP 3** mail rather than a web based system. (See Chapter 6.)

2.   If you opt for a service with a fee, use free trials before signing up

There can be a significant difference between different ISPs and many offer a range of subscription packages. Be wary of committing yourself to one provider for a long time, this is an area of rapidly changing costs and offers.

3.   Investigate call discount schemes

Check on telecom company offers of free off peak Internet calls. If you pay for local calls, check whether your phone company offers discounts on frequently called numbers and add the ISP's Internet access number to it. Where a phone company is also offering Internet access they may offer discounted calls to customers using their system.

4.   Use the Internet when it's cheap and fast

Access the web during cheap rate for phone calls and connect at times that are not busy. This varies depending where you live, but it's basically governed by whether the USA is asleep or awake. At busy times you may fail to make connections and data transfer will be slower.

5.   Access sites through favourites

Create favourites offline so that time on line is not spent typing in long URLs. Have the ones you want to visit at the top of your favourites file.

6. **Avoid slow loading home pages**
   A site's home page is not always the best one to select as your future starting point. Many take a long time to load. Subsequent pages are usually plainer and give access to the rest of the site.

7. **Set your home page as a blank**
   It means your computer won't try to dial up every time you open your browser. The home page of your ISP can be slow to load and may not be the place you always want to start from.

8. **Stop images, sound and video clips being loaded automatically**
   Set your browser not to include these and pages will take less time to load.

9. **Don't try to read information on screen**
   Go quickly to any links that interest you, your eye will be drawn to them because they are coloured and underlined text or pictures. Watch the status bar which tells you what's happening with your connections and data transfer. Once it says Done, or words to that effect, it has cached the link you requested and you can go back to where you started using the **back** button. Read and print pages offline using history or offline browsing facilities.

10. **Compose all your email messages offline and send several at a time**
    Most email software lets you store messages in an out tray. No matter how many messages and how diverse their destinations, they will all be sent as part of the same phone call. Use the address book facility to store

frequently used addresses.

11. **Copy and paste email for web based accounts**

    If you are using a web based email account and cannot compose offline, write your message using a word processing package, copy it to the clipboard. Then go on line, access your email site and paste the message in.

12. **Plan ahead**

    Have a clear idea of what you hope to get from a session on the Internet before you connect. Have emails ready to send and sites to visit in **favourites**. If you know that you're likely to get carried away, set a timer to jolt you out of your absorption.

13. **Keep an eye on downloads**

    When downloading software check the size of the files and the time the transfer is likely to take. Don't go away and leave a long download, keep checking that data is coming through and that the clock is counting down. If something goes wrong, the data transfer can stop, but you are still paying for the telephone connection.

14. **Only use the Internet when it's appropriate**

    Don't assume that the Internet is the best way to research everything.

15. **Give up when you're losing**

    Both telephones and computers are a wonderful tools when they work properly, and sources of immense frustration when they don't. There will inevitably be times when things go wrong. If things aren't working properly, it's a good idea to take a break. It may be fixed by the time you come back.

MAKING WHAT MATTERS WORK FOR YOU

✓ Download UnMozify from **http://www.evolve.co.uk** then work offline on previously visited web sites to try out making changes to your browser appearance and to familiarise yourself with right button options.

✓ Try out the Print Target and Save Target commands. You can only do this offline if you did previously visit that link.

✓ Download Adobe and Winzip to enable you to open documents and programs you'll be helping yourself to in future.
http://www.adobe.com
http://www.winzip.com/download/htm

✓ Take a look at the range of freeware and shareware that's on offer
http://www.download.com
http://tucows.cableinet.net

✓ Compare current telecom company deals for local call costs and discount schemes. Check that ISP numbers can be included in any discounts.

5 Effective Searching

Knowing where to look starts to make the
Internet a manageable place.

3

things that
really matter

New Internet users can feel overwhelmed and daunted by the volume of material on the web. When you're inundated with information, much of which is irrelevant, it can seem impossible to find exactly what you want. We use indexes, catalogues and recommendations to select what we read and watch; similar systems exist on the Internet.

Unlike other libraries of information there is no single classification system on the World Wide Web. **Search engines**, **directories** and **meta searchers** act as index and contents pages for web information. They are powerful tools that can help you find what you want. Many have enthusiastic sounding names like **Yahoo!**, **Yell** and **Excite**; they behave in an enthusiastic manner, quickly fetching lots of interesting things for you to look at. The number of matches they return can be daunting, but often what you want is at the top of the list. A less haphazard way to get what you want is to understand what search tools are and how they work.

IS THIS YOU?

• *Frustrated by getting millions of mostly irrelevant matches to a query.* • *Unsure of how to use search tools other than those on your toolbar button.*

• *Unable to find anything at all on an obscure subject.*

• *Uncertain which search engine to use.* • *Confused by the different ways of entering search phrases.* • *Wanting to search the web sites of just one country.* • *Needing to translate a web page.*

AltaVista™   **Results**   Help - AltaVista Home

Ask AltaVista™ a question. Or enter a few words in [any language ▾]   Advanced

[help with essays on shakepeares hamlet]   [Search]

▸ AltaVista found about 7,043,789 Web pages for you. Refine your search

1. **Need help with Hamlet essay**
   Replies | Post Reply | Shakespeare Queries From Genuinely Interested Students 3.15.97:
   Top | Help. Need help with Hamlet essay. This is the question...
   URL: www.shakespeare.com/qandr/students/3.15....ssages/766.html
   Last modified 1-Apr-97 - page size 4K - in English [Translate]

2. **traps found within HAMLET**
   Replies | Post Reply | Shakespeare Queries From Lazy or Unwilling Students 3.15.97: Top |
   Help. traps found within HAMLET. Please help me with the...
   URL: www.shakespeare.com/qandr/lazy/3.15.97/messages/266.html
   Last modified 21-Mar-97 - page size 3K - in English [Translate]

3. **HAMLET AS A TRAGIC HERO**
   Replies | Post Reply | Shakespeare Queries From Genuinely Interested Students 3.15.97:
   Top | Help. HAMLET AS A TRAGIC HERO. HAMLET AS A TRAGIC HERO....
   URL: www.shakespeare.com/qandr/students/3.15.97/messages/26.html
   Last modified 30-Mar-97 - page size 3K - in English [Translate]

4. **What do Oedipus and Hamlet have in common?**

AltaVista is a powerful search tool.

 ## KNOWING WHERE TO LOOK

Your **search button** links to some **search tools** but you don't have to use just these. They have been selected by your provider for commercial reasons and may not be the best tool for all your searches. Different directories and search engines are good for different things. Try the same searches with a few to see which gives the best results for your queries.

Directories are compiled by humans with sites being assigned to appropriate sections. This means you can browse by category as well as entering key words for a search. Although this cuts down on irrelevant matches, directories can be small and give less comprehensive results than **search engines**. These run automatically visiting a huge number of web sites and newsgroups, constantly updating their content. They search on word match rather than context and this can result in a lot of irrelevant documents.

A good way to find which search tool is producing the bests results for a specific query is to use a meta search tool like Dogpile **http://www.dogpile.com** This sends your query to 24 searchers at once and then shows you the results. It's not unusual to have a query where one search engine returns no matches whilst another finds hundreds. Dogpile is a quick way to find which are likely to deal best with your particular query. You can even arrange the order in which your queries are sent to search tools. Like all search tools Dogpile has an excellent help section that explain in detail how it all works. Perhaps its most useful advice is:

If you still do not understand any of this, don't worry. Just try it and see what happens.

At the other end of the scale from these huge searchers are more specific ones. These can be useful if you want to limit your search to a geographical area or particular providers such as universities or medical organisations.

Geographically specific resources concentrate on a particular area of the world. Large directories such as Yahoo! have country specific sections. Most countries and continents have search tools that are specific to them, e.g. Euroferret **http://www.euroferret.com**, UK Max **http://www.ukmax.com**, UK Plus **http://www.ukplus.co.uk**

Some combine geographical selection with other criteria. The Academic Directory **http://acdc.hensa.ac.uk** has the option to search web pages from the UK Academic Internet only.

Subject gateways compiled and maintained by universities and professional organisations offer access to subject expertise world wide.

EEVL

Edinburgh Engineering Virtual Library

The UK gateway to quality engineering information on the Internet

EEVL helps engineers to find relevant information on the Internet by maintaining a searchable catalogue of reviews and links to quality engineering Web sites, and provides targeted engineering search engines, indexes to print literature and other specialist information services.

▲ Search EEVL Catalogue
Reviews of 3,600 quality engineering Web sites. Use BROAD search terms for the best results. Updated daily.

▲ Search UK Engineering Web Sites
Relevant engineering Web sites selected by EEVL. Use NARROW search terms.

▲ Search Engineering E-journals 🎖️
Over 100 engineering e-journal Web sites: articles, news, product reviews.

▲ Search Engineering Newsgroups
40 day archive.

▲ Submit a Site to EEVL

▲ Browse EEVL Catalogue by Subject
Reviews of 3,600 quality engineering Web sites.

▲ Browse EEVL Catalogue by Resource Type
Web sites classified by type - e-journals, companies, recruitment agencies, societies etc.

▲ What's New
Latest additions to the EEVL Catalogue.

▲ September UK Top 25 🎖️
The most visited sites in the .uk domain.

▲ September Top 25 🎖️
The most visited sites worldwide.

▲ EEVL's All-Time Top 250
The most visited sites worldwide.

EEVL http://www.eevl.ac.uk allows you to target quality engineering resources that have been compiled and evaluated by experts.

For some types of information, academic sites are a good starting point. As well as providing comprehensive, accurate up to date information they will have links to other sites considered worthwhile. Excellent starting points for this are:

- **The Pinakes**, once the name given to the catalogue of the Library at Alexandria this provides a gateway to the academic Internet. **http://www.hw.ac.uk/libWWW/irn/ pinakes/pinakes.html**

- **BUBL** acts as an information service for the UK academic community. There are links from here to sites dealing with all subjects
  http://www.bubl.ac.uk

- **The scholarly societies** project from a Canadian university lists and provides links to scholarly societies on every subject everywhere in the world.
  http://www.lib.uwaterloo.ca/society/overview.html

Web guides

You often choose a book, film or a play on the recommendations of others. On the web there's no shortage of guides that review sites. These can be from media organisations such as the BBC, student groups, organisations promoting family use of the Internet or on an individual's personal site. Home pages of Internet Service Providers and search engines often include a guide section under headings like What's New or What's Cool. Newspapers like *The Guardian* **http://www. guardian.co.uk** have site review sections and archive these on their own web sites.

Such guides are useful as a general introduction to the Internet as they highlight sites that are worthwhile. Guides differ from other search tools in that they make judgements on the quality of the information. Inclusion of a web site is a recommendation of it. BBC Education for example has a web guide **http://www.bbc.co.uk/education/webguide** that is compiled and reviewed by subject specialists. As with the academic gateways, why start from scratch when you can use the findings of others with more time, experience and expertise!

 LEARNING HOW TO LOOK

Language is full of ambiguities that are not always understood by computer searches. As well as using the right search site you've got to think of how to put keywords together to help the search tool recognise what you're really looking for. Many searchers allow you to narrow your search and include or exclude things with, for example, the simple option of matching **any** or **all of your words**. Details are in their help sections. Different tools allow different options for refining a search.

If you're getting too many or too few matches, take time to look at these help sections. A common way is using words in the following:

Simple keyword search query:

Appalachian:

This query will return all objects containing the word **Appalachian**.

Boolean query:

Appalachian AND mountains.

This query will return all objects that contain **both words** anywhere in the object in any order.

Negated query:

Appalachian AND NOT mountains.

This query will return all objects that contain the word **Appalachian** and don't contain the word **mountains**.
Phrase query:

"Appalachian mountains".

This query will return all objects that contain **Appalachian mountains** as a phrase.

If you use a meta searcher it will attempt to translate your search syntax to that which will be recognised by each engine it sends to.

Search tools like AltaVista **http://www.altavista.com** and Ask Jeeves! **http://www.aj.com** allow you to ask a question in plain English then offer a range of topics to be searched for. This allows you to see how your words are being interpreted. Here in response to the question **How do bees fly?** it has understood that the searcher is interested in bees

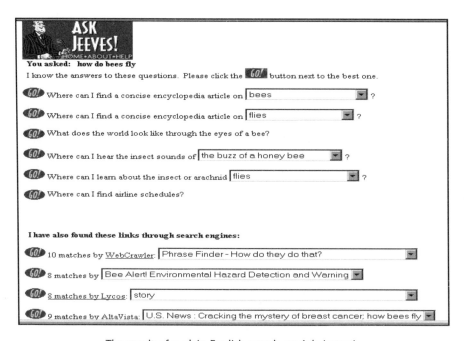

The result of a plain English search on Ask Jeeves!

and most options relate to this, but has also offered links to information on flies and airline schedules.

If you get a page of results and feel you'd like to look at all of them, set it as your home page. Follow links, then get back to the original easily just by clicking the home button.

 MAKING SEARCH TOOLS WORK FOR YOU

Search sites do more than just search. They are all trying to attract visitors so they can boast of a huge number of users to advertisers. They do this by offering something extra that they hope will bring users back and often try to gather information about you in the process. Most have a clear privacy policy and undertake not to sell your details on to their advertisers. There is of course nothing to stop you inventing identities for the purpose of registering with such sites.

You can personalise search site home pages so they reflect your interests, get free email accounts, subscribe to newsletters which keep you updated on for example latest news headlines, TV listings or lottery results.

One of the nicest extras is the translation option from AltaVista. You can use it to translate a phrase or letter of your own or for whole web pages. The translation service is at **http://babelfish.altavista.com** or select the **translate** option which appears with AltaVista search results.

MAKING WHAT MATTERS WORK FOR YOU

✓ Try all the search and guide sites mentioned in this chapter with the same query and see the different results.
http://acdc.hensa.ac.uk
http://www.aj.com
http://www.altavista.com
http://www.bbc.co.uk/education/webguide
http://www.bubl.ac.uk
http://www.dogpile.com
http://www.eevl.ac.uk
http://www.euroferret.com
http://www.excite.com
http://www.guardian.co.uk
http://www.hw.ac.uk/libWWW/irn/pinakes/pinakes.html
http://www.ukmax.com
http://www.ukplus.co.uk
http://www.yahoo.co.uk
http://www.yahoo.com
Print off the help sections and advanced searching tips from the search tools you like best.

✓ Experiment with including and excluding words from searches and see how it affects your results. Try enclosing your search phrase in " " and compare those results with a search of the same phrase without inverted commas.

✓ Personalise Yahoo! or Excite to see how it works.

✓ Look at **http://www.searchenginewatch.com** to compare search tools, find out more about searching the web or access tutorials on searching. Register for a free e-mail newsletter to keep you up to date with search tool developments.

6 Email

*Email is the Internet's postal service and its most
popular facility.*

This cheap and efficient way of keeping in touch is
deservedly popular. As well as letters, you can send and
receive all types of files or join in discussions with people
who share your interests through **mailing lists**. Your
connection with an Internet Service Provider will normally
include email software and mailboxes.

There are lots of services which offer **free email** which
can be web based or make use of your existing mail
software. Such software includes features to manage your
correspondence. Web based email directories help you find
elusive addresses.

Email software is free, easy to use and helps you keep
your correspondence organised.

IS THIS YOU?

• Keen to keep in touch with friends and family who live all over the world. • Wanting to send documents and pictures to others. • Worried about making your email address known in case you get junk mail. • Interested in setting up different email accounts for different purposes. • Not sure how to get the best out of your email software. • Uncertain of how to compose and read email offline. • Wondering how to check email on your home account when you're away • Trying to find the email for someone you've lost touch with.

EMAIL ADDRESSES

When you set up your Internet account you will normally get at least one mailbox and email address.

A typical address will look like:

- **aunty@freemail.com**
- **irene@serviceprovider.net**
- **ik@essentials.freeserve.co.uk**

Email addresses are similar to URLs and require the same attention to accuracy.

- The first part of the address is the name you choose for yourself. It may not always be your first name or initials because once a name has been allocated, it cannot be used by anyone else. If the name you want has been taken, you have to use a certain amount of imagination and ingenuity in choosing another to represent you.
- Your name is always followed by @ (at).
- With some providers like Freeserve you need to choose an additional account name that will come after the @ and before their domain name. This account name has to be unique, and you need to think of alternatives if your

first choice has been spoken for.

- The final part shows who your account is with and follows the same conventions as URLs.

Many ISPs give you more than one address and there's no limit to the number of free ones you can use.

② USING FREE EMAIL, FORWARDING ACCOUNTS AND POP GATEWAYS

Re-invent yourself with a new email personality.

If you don't have an Internet account, or frequently change providers, there are several companies offering different types of **free email accounts**. You can have a:

- **POP 3** account which uses your existing mail software.

- **Web based mail** which is accessed through a web site and does not need mail software.

- **Forwarding account** which sends your email to any other account you choose.

You can of course have all of these plus your regular ISP account and use each for different purposes.

POP stands for **Post Office Protocol** and is the way your software communicates with mail servers. To read this type of mail you need a standard **Internet POP-client**, such as Outlook Express, Eudora, Pegasus Mail or Netscape Mail. This is the type of account you normally get from your ISP.

Incoming messages are stored on a server and remain there until you connect and download the messages to your computer. The big advantage of this is that you can write and read messages off line and use your software package to organise your mail.

The main disadvantage was that until recently you could

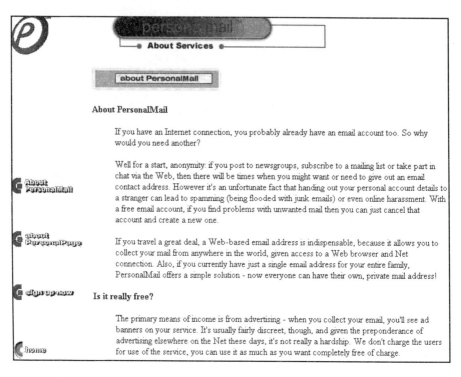

About PersonalMail

If you have an Internet connection, you probably already have an email account too. So why would you need another?

Well for a start, anonymity: if you post to newsgroups, subscribe to a mailing list or take part in chat via the Web, then there will be times when you might want or need to give out an email contact address. However it's an unfortunate fact that handing out your personal account details to a stranger can lead to spamming (being flooded with junk emails) or even online harassment. With a free email account, if you find problems with unwanted mail then you can just cancel that account and create a new one.

If you travel a great deal, a Web-based email address is indispensable, because it allows you to collect your mail from anywhere in the world, given access to a Web browser and Net connection. Also, if you currently have just a single email address for your entire family, PersonalMail offers a simple solution - now everyone can have their own, private mail address!

Is it really free?

The primary means of income is from advertising - when you collect your email, you'll see ad banners on your service. It's usually fairly discreet, though, and given the preponderance of advertising elsewhere on the Net these days, it's not really a hardship. We don't charge the users for use of the service, you can use it as much as you want completely free of charge.

Take a look at free POP accounts offered by http://www.pmail.net

only access your email easily from a computer configured to connect to your mail server. Now web based **POP gateway** services enable you to read your email from anywhere with a web connection (see page 65).

Web based email enables you to log into a web site to access your email. This means that mail has to be composed, read and organised whilst you are online. If you want to keep messages there is usually a folder facility. Messages can be printed, saved or copied. Different web based free email services come with different tools, such as spell-checkers, address books and folder systems. There are hundreds of such services, one of the best known is Hotmail **http://www.hotmail.com** To find other services take a look at **http://www.emailaddresses.com.**

Forwarding services automatically send on mail from your free address to any email address you nominate. The result is that you can have one email address that will not change regardless of how many times you change provider. You can alter where your mail is forwarded to easily or choose to leave it in a web based post box.

The domain names offered by free services are often much more individual than those you get from your ISP. You can set up different ones for different purposes, depending on the impression you want to create like ducky@quack quack.com, busy@notme.com or hardworking@alltimes.com.

Is there a catch? Not really, they are collecting any personal information you choose to give them and may sell this on to advertisers. Some forwarding services may make their more attractive addresses free for a limited period only, others are free for ever, or as long as that company stays in business. Web based free email is financed by the advertising you see on sites, but in my case twelve free addresses have not led to excessive junk mail. Some companies and ISPs may block emails from certain free addresses because of worries that junk mailers and crooks can hide behind the anonymity such addresses offer.

If you set up several mail accounts, keep a record of addresses and password for each!

POP3 gateway services like **http://www.emailbooth.com** act as a way of accessing your POP3 account from any computer. You need to know your login name, password and mail server address. Details will be shown on your dial up connection, or check with your provider.

Junk mail, or **spam** as it's often called, wastes time, clutters up your mailbox and costs because you go online

Welcome to EmailBooth

Welcome to **EmailBooth** check and send Email from Your Pop3
E-mail account anywhere on the Web...
To check your mail now, login here: **Help**

Login: | irene |
Password: | ✱✱✱✱✱✱ |
Server: | mail.providername.net |

☐ Check here to use an interface that does not make use of frames, for older or smaller web browsers. The frames interface requires a browser that supports cookies as well as frames.

☑ Check here to expire EmailBooth output, for increased security and privacy.

[LOG IN]

to receive it. However, people can only send you junk mail if they know your address. If you have your own web pages you will almost inevitably attract some junk mailers. With most mail programs you can stop messages with characteristics you choose ever being downloaded (see the section below on filtering).

You can stipulate addresses that you reject email from, or delete emails with particular phrases such as *make money fast* – a common subject line for junk mail – from the server.

Another way of getting spam is to post to a newsgroup. Spammers use automated systems to collect email addresses from such postings. Extra mail boxes and free accounts are useful here. If you want to join in a discussion and subsequently find it results in repeated junk mail you can abandon that address.

 SENDING AND RECEIVING MAIL AND ATTACHMENTS

Once you've set your account up you can send and receive email. Details here are shown using Microsoft's **Outlook Express**. The features described are common to most programs but may have different names and buttons.

Email software can be explored and manipulated offline

so spend time trying out the different commands and facilities. Don't ignore the help section of your email program but use it to experiment with different settings. You can change almost every facet of your email program if you want to!

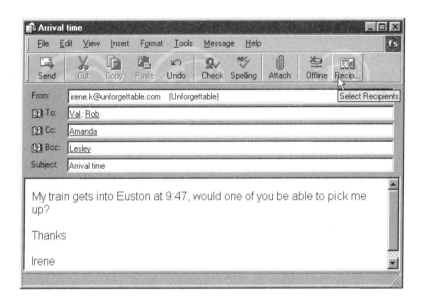

A typical mail composition window.

Familiarise yourself with the following essentials:

The **new mail** window in which you compose your email. This always has a space for the addresses of recipients. You can send multiple copies by putting all names in the **To:** or the **Cc:** (copy) section. Addresses are usually separated from each other by a semi colon. Emails sent like this show each recipient who else is on the list.

If you enter names in the **Bcc:** section this sends a **blind copy** to those listed. Recipients do not see who else copies have been sent to, but the email arrives addressed to the person in the **To:** box. Filling in the subject line is important as your recipient is likely to just see the name of the sender and the subject of the email. If they get a lot of unsolicited mail you need to make the subject line interesting enough not to be overlooked.

The **menu bar** and **toolbar** commands allow you to carry out a range of functions similar to those in browser and word processing packages.

You will find commands that let you:

- choose whether to send your message immediately or later,
- change the identity of the sender,
- set the priority of a message,
- vary the stationery you use,
- cut, copy and paste,
- delete,
- check your spelling,
- insert files as attachments, and
- search your messages.

There are different commands available when composing, reading and managing your mail and toolbars can be customised. Don't be afraid to experiment with them.

Any file on your computer can be inserted and sent as attachments with your email. All mail programs have an **Insert** command or icon. This brings up the **Insert Attachment** box from which you choose the files you wish to send. Check that your recipient has software that can read it. If for example you send a Word 97 document to someone who has Word 6 the formatting will be lost and replaced by gobbledygook. When sending a large file it is considerate to zip it first so that it takes less time to transmit, but this only works if the recipient has an unzip program.

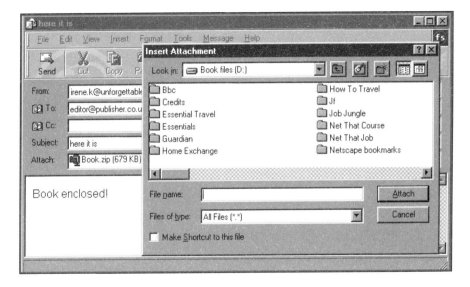

Remember to virus check attachments before opening them.

 KEEPING ORGANISED

Email is so quick and easy you'll find you're sending and receiving hundreds.

A little time spent familiarising yourself with tools to manage mail and customising your system will pay dividends later. The most useful functions include:

- An **address book** that stores commonly used addresses for you. Some programs automatically add the address of anyone you send an email to.

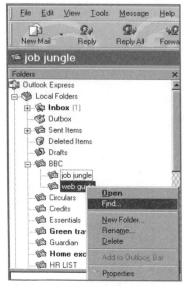

The number of unread messages in a folder is shown next to it.

- A **folder** system to help you organise messages. The first four folders here are pre-set but you can add as many extra ones as you need. To add a new folder, go to **file/folders** and choose **new ...** Once you have created a new folder clicking with the right button of the mouse on it brings up a menu box allowing you to make alterations or add sub folders.

  New messages are filed in your Inbox. Messages you have composed are stored in the Outbox until you connect. Deleted messages are stored in the **deleted items** folder until you empty it.

- A **search** facility, accessed here from **edit** in the **menu bar**. Even if you carefully file your messages away it can be difficult to find the one you want.

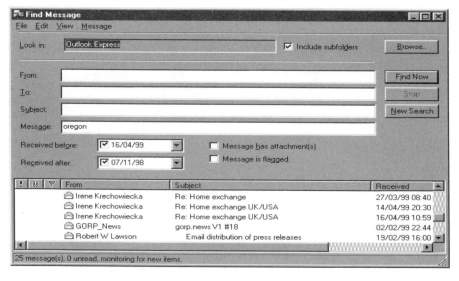

Being able to search on a word, the author or subject of a message is a quick way of getting to the right place.

- A **message filtering** system, in Outlook Express this is accessed through **tools/message rules** on the initial window menu bar. You can limit the size of messages you accept, delete messages from undesirable correspondents, send an automated reply if you're away or forward mail elsewhere.

Once you are confident about using all the above explore how to alter settings using **tools/options ...** This allows you to modify the way your email looks and behaves.

 FINDING ADDRESSES

You can look up email addresses in the same way as you search for web sites, often using the same tools. Like other searches the results vary. People Search **http://peoplesearch.net** which sends to four search engines at once, found six of my twelve addresses. Each address was different, and they did all belong to me!

MAKING WHAT MATTERS WORK FOR YOU

✓ Find information on and links to every type of email account at
http://www.emailaddresses.com

✓ Set up web based email accounts that will also act as forwarders and
try:
http://www.bigfoot.com
http://www.iname.com
http://www.myownemail.com
http://www.netforward.com

✓ To set up new POP 3 account try:
http://www.pmail.net
http://www.popaccount.com

✓ Find yourself or a long lost friend using People Search
http://www.peoplesearch.net

✓ Experiment with your settings, options and filtering systems by sending
emails to yourself at the new accounts you've set up before unleashing
your new found skills on the wider world.

✓ Create folders to organise emails you want to keep.

✓ Check your home email account from another computer using:
http://www.emailbooth.com
http://www.twigger.com

7 Mailing Lists and Newsgroups

Join in a discussion, there's thousands to choose from!

1 FINDING AND USING MAILING LISTS

2 FINDING THE RIGHT NEWSGROUPS

things that
really matter

Newsgroups and mailing lists give you the chance to listen into or join discussions on any topic that interests you. They're an easy way of connecting with people who share your interests.

Access to newsgroups can be through your ISP, using news reading software that is similar to what you use for email. With **Outlook Express** newsreading comes as part of the mail program. Mailing lists are a way of conducting group discussions using email and do not require additional software.

It's also possible to participate in newsgroup discussions through web sites like **Deja News** which offer web based reading and posting facilities.

IS THIS YOU?

• Looking for others who share your interests?
• Needing regularly updated information on a subject? • Searching for an answer to a niggling question? • Unsure of what subscribing to newsletters, mailing lists or newsgroups means? • Don't know where to start looking for discussions that interest you? • Worried about filling your mail box with junk?

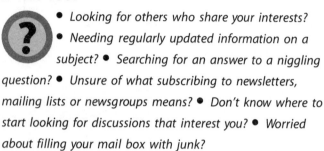

① FINDING AND USING MAILING LISTS

If you join a mailing list you will have discussions posted to you as emails. Choose whether to just observe, reply to the whole list or individuals. The number of emails you get depends on the popularity of the list. Be selective or you'll end up with an overflowing post box.

To find information on mailing lists, use dedicated search tools such as:

http://www.liszt.com

http://www.neosoft.com/internet/paml

http://www.mailbase.ac.uk

These sites give details of how to join a list. This is normally done by sending an email with a message such as *subscribe* followed by the name of the list you wish to receive.

Once you sign up for a list you'll receive a confirmation and details of how to cancel or **unsubscribe**. It's important to keep this so that you can leave the list. Messages sent to the list should add to the debate as they are distributed to all list members. The address you send an unsubscribe command to is always different from the one you send messages to.

Unsubscribe from mailing lists if you're going to be away

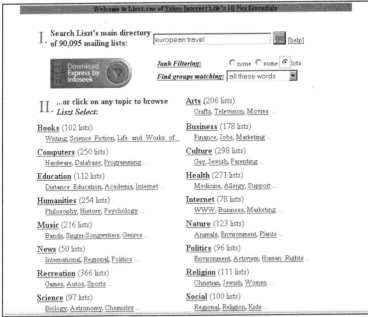

There's a mailing list on just about everything.

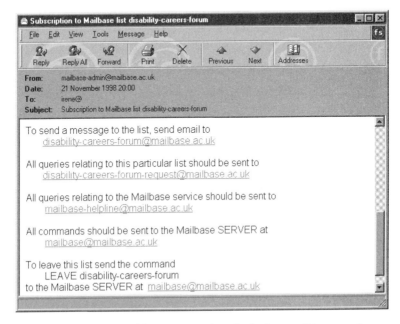

An easy and very public way to make a fool of yourself is to send
an unsubscribe message to everyone on the list.

for some time, otherwise you'll come back to thousands of messages clogging up your post box.

Mailing lists can be **closed** or **open, moderated** or **unmoderated**:

- Closed mailing lists only send information to you.

- Open mailing lists allow you to contribute to the discussion and can be:

  – unmoderated lists – automatically display all messages   posted

     – moderated lists – someone checks the suitability of   messages and decides which to include.

Moderation can be useful because it prevents irrelevant, offensive or advertising material creeping in. Most people who act as moderators of lists are unpaid and do it for the love of the subject. Don't try their patience by posting inappropriately.

Electronic newsletters are a variation on newsgroups and mailing lists. They come as email and can be subscribed to from the organisation's web site. Examples include:

- Scambusters – helps you keep up with what to avoid from the Internet
  http://www.scambusters.org

- Smart parent – dedicated to educating parents on how to safeguard their children from the dangers of the Internet
  http://www.smartparent.com

- 1ski – weekly update on all matters ski related
  http://www.1Ski.com

- Rough guides – updates on travel related issues
  http://travel.roughguides.com

- Cool works – information on jobs in national parks, ski resorts and other wonderful places in the USA
http://www.coolworks.com

 FINDING THE RIGHT NEWSGROUPS

Newsgroups are 'places' where people with similar interests exchange views, ask questions, offer help and occasionally bicker and insult each other. They are a source of information, amusement and occasionally frustration. Contributors can be experts in their field or weird eccentrics and you should take the same precautions as you would with all other parts of the Internet. The newsgroups you can subscribe to through your news reading software depend on what your ISP makes available, usually a choice of around 30,000.

Subscribing to newsgroups is free. News reading software generally comes with mail software and is similar to it. You can compose and read previously collected

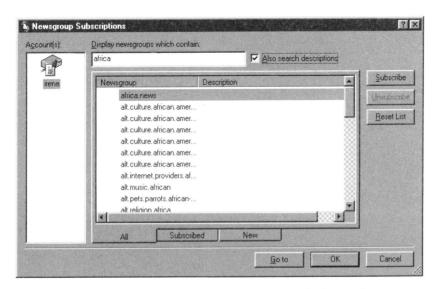

There is usually a facility to search newsgroups by keyword.

messages offline. You need to go on line to receive the full list of newsgroups kept by your ISP. Receiving this takes a few minutes, but then you can look at and search it offline.

Subscribing and unsubscribing are fully explained in the help section of the software. Once you subscribe, new articles will be posted to you and can be collected each time you go on line in the same way as you collect mail. You can of course read them offline. There may be hundreds of

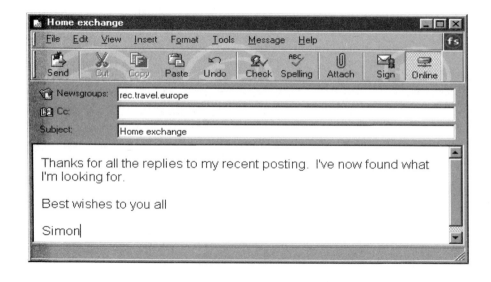

Posting to newsgroups is like sending an email.

new articles each day for any one newsgroup, so avoid the temptation to subscribe to too many. To save time download message headers only and then get the full text of anything interesting later.

Each **newsgroup** has a unique **name** made up of several parts which give an indication of the subjects they are dealing with. The first part of the name tells you which category it comes into. Some of the common ones are:

- **alt.** – alternative newsgroups, informal and unofficial information,
- **biz.** – commercial and business matters,
- **comp.** – computer related discussion,
- **misc.** – catch all for subjects that don't fit anywhere else,
- **sci.** – scientific discussion,
- **rec.** – recreational interests, and
- **soc.** – discussions on cultural, social and religious issues.

The second part of the name gives you an indication of the specific subject they're dealing with. For example :

- alt.comics.superman
- biz.jobs.offered
- comp.bugs.misc
- misc.news.bosnia
- rec.arts.dance
- sci.geo.geology
- soc.religion.eastern

Most search engines have a facility to **find information** from and about newsgroups, so you can find information on a topic in newsgroups as well as on web sites. Search tools like Deja News **http://www.deja.com** specialise in newsgroups. It's possible to search either on a subject or the name of the person sending information. If you register with Deja News you can read from, and post to, newsgroups through the site. They even provide a free email address to do it with. This gives access to over 80,000 discussion groups. It's a free service rather like web based email and it means you don't need an Internet account or news reading software. However, all your reading and posting is done on-line.

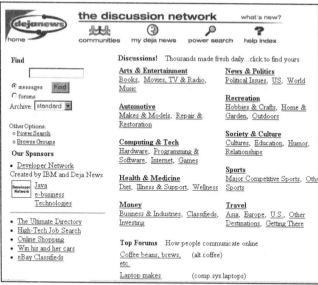

Use Deja to find discussions that match your interests.

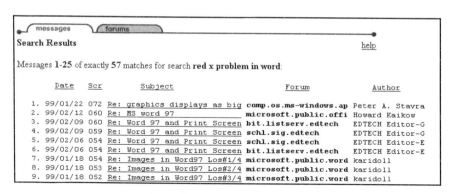

Archived messages can hold answers and solutions to seemingly insurmountable problems and help you identify groups it may be useful to subscribe to.

MAKING WHAT MATTERS WORK FOR YOU

✓ Use the mailing list search sites in this chapter to find lists that interest you. Subscribe to one or two initially to see how much email it generates. Make a new folder in your mail program to store messages you want to keep from lists. Make sure you save the unsubscribe details.

✓ Investigate your newsreading software. The help section will show you how to receive the initial list of groups available from your provider. Subscribe to one or two newsgroups. Use **tools/message rules** to receive only recent postings. This keeps the number of messages manageable.

✓ Experiment with receiving message headers only and then marking those that look interesting for later retrieval. Commands for this are in **tools/synchronize**.

✓ Use Deja News **http://www.deja.com** to see the full range of groups for topics that interests you and to read archived discussions.

MAKING WHAT MATTERS WORK FOR YOU

- Compare prices for something you're buying — http://www.buy.co.uk
- Plan a journey — http://www.euroshell.com
- Research a holiday destination — http://www.lonelyplanet.com
- Understand your computer — http://www.microsoft.com
- Check a health issue — http://www.nlm.nih.gov
- Compare public services in your area with the rest of the country — http://www.upmystreet.com
- Find people with similar interests or problems to yours — http://www.dejanews.com
- Check the latest news — http://www.bbc.co.uk
- Get help with homework — http://www.launchsite.org
- Find another job — http://www.jobsunlimited.co.uk
- Move house — http://www.virtualrelocation.com
- Give an effective presentation — http://www.kumc.edu/SAH/OTEd/jradel/effective.html
- Manage your finances — http://www.fool.co.uk
- Translate something to or from another language — http://babelfish.altavista.com
- Check the weather at home or in another part of the world — http://www.meto.gov.uk
- Fill in your tax return — http://www.inlandrevenue.gov.uk
- Find a course at a UK university — http://www.ucas.ac.uk
- Get help with job search and application techniques — http://www.bbc.co.uk/education/workskills/jobs/index. shtml
- Arrange a home exchange — http://www.swapnow.com
- Find out which destinations to avoid — http://www.fco.gov.uk
- Get detailed UK maps — http://www.multimap.com

- Search for a phone number   http://www.bt.com/phonenet.uk
- Learn a new language   http://www.travlang.com
- Check out what's on anywhere in the world   http://www.eventsworldwide.com
- Help in the search for extraterrestrial intelligence   http://setiathome.ssl.berkeley.edu
- Get driving directions for places in the US   http://www.mapblast.com
- Find out about living, working and studying around the EU   http://citizens.eu.int
- Check out disability issues   http://www.disability.org.uk
- Find out who's polluting you   http://www.foe.co.uk/factorywatch
- Investigate a legal problem   http://www.lawrights.co.uk
- Learn how everything works   http://www.howstuffworks.com
- Read the world's newspapers   http://www.mediainfo.com/emedia
- Take part in a virtual auction   http://www.ebay.com
- Visit Mars   http://www.nasa.gov
- Find out how to work for MI5   http://www.mi5.gov.uk
- Find work in a beautiful place   http://www.coolworks.com
- Get ski reports and piste maps   htt://www.1ski.com
- Check your employment rights   http://www.tuc.org.uk
- Visit one of the best garden centres   http://www.rhs.org.uk
- Learn to cope with bullies   http://www.successunlimited.co.uk
- Find the right word   http://www.dictionary.com
- Buy and sell a car   http://www.carseller.co.uk
- Find a last minute holiday   http://www.instant-holidays.com
- Read the latest UK business stories   http://www.ukbusinesspark.co.uk
- Find a job in film or TV production   http://www.mandy.com
- Go to the dogs   http://www.the-kennel-club.org.uk
- Investigate a learning holiday   http://www.aredu.demon.co.uk
- Find a recipe   http://www.culinary-resource.co.uk